The 7-Figure Introvert

By Val Neighbors

Book Dedication

This book is dedicated to all the introverts in the world who know they can serve the world in a bigger way and are scared to death of what it means. You can and will do it with grace and ease and the support of us other introverts who have already started the journey. You've got this and we've got your back.

Introduction

If you've seen me on stage or camera, you may have thought I was an extrovert, when in fact I am an introvert who learned to conform to an extroverted world. I want to share how you as an introvert can actually have a more impactful and dynamic seven figure business. Now I know what you are thinking, a lot of times when we think of the person that is the successful business owner, we think of extroverts. The truth of the matter is that I found in my own life, through the successes that I've had, that being an introvert now more of an ambivert, that personality played a huge role in what I have accomplished.

Most of my life I always thought that I was an extrovert. To the point where at times I almost felt like I was an overcompensating extrovert. Taking my personality to the extreme of being introverted. Then other times I felt like I was always acting as though I was saying, "Hey look at me, hey look at me, hey look at me!"

Over the past year I started to get quiet with myself and slow myself down, not necessarily by choice. As I was reflecting upon my life up until now, I realized that from kindergarten until my senior year in high school, I went to 6 different schools. Now that may not seem like a lot, but the impact of moving away from my core group of friends and in to new situations meant I was always starting over.

Because I moved so many times and I was constantly the new kid coming in to an environment of established friendships and relationships. Let's face it, kids don't necessarily embrace the new kid with welcome and open arms, especially at different age brackets. I quickly figured out that I either had to be the person that forced myself outside of my comfort zone and engage in the conversation or I had to be the first one to say "Hi", in order to make some friends and have some level of acceptance.

If I had been completely quiet and not said a word I would have always continued to be the the outcast. Obviously I chose path A of pushing myself out of my comfort zone and be the one to initiate conversation. So, now as an adult it comes natural to me. That doesn't mean I am an extrovert.

Sitting Back

I understand now that me being an introvert is actually a positive thing, not negative. Now with that said, I want you to know that I thought for the longest time with the successes that I was having, I was having it living as though I was an extrovert. I was out there. I was succeeding and because of that, I identified myself as being an extrovert. How many of us have been through that where we are introverts but we have spent a lot of time living as an extrovert because of the situations that we are put into?

A perfect example of that might be the stereotypical networking event. If you are like me in business, you've probably been to a lot of networking events. I've got to tell you honestly that networking events wear me out. It's not that I have difficulty meeting with people. It's not, as so many people wrongly define it, that being an introvert means I'm shy. In fact, being outgoing comes very easy to me. But it does mean it drains my energy, unlike an extrovert who a group situation would energize.

So, what I have learned is how to sit back and observe. I fought sitting and being quiet for so many years. What I have found is that I really have begun to develop the power that comes from embracing who I am. Even in networking meetings where at the end of it I honestly just need a chance to be able to rest, to sit back and to be drained like events do to introverts.

Introvert Impact

The thing we have to realize is that half the population are introverts and the world needs them. Really introverts tend to make better managers because they are good at observing, listening, and asking questions. These are three of the best qualities in a manager.

Unfortunately, a lot of times they find themselves getting

passed up for promotions because they don't know how to leverage their talents rather than listening, observing and then adding impactful information into the environment. They are just seen as that person that is over there being quiet. So that is my #1 mission to help introverts use their skills in business.

Because sales is so near and dear to my heart my #2 mission is help people understand that a good sales person is NOT a person that talks all the time. The truth of the matter is that sales is very much about listening. It's not about how much you can talk. Sales is about being a person who adds the right questions to help determine what their needs are, what their pains are, so that hopefully you can present a solution.

Whether it's a product or service that you currently represent, or a recommendation out to somebody else who can help them, sales is about solutions. Sales are about making somebody look good and making their life easier. Introverts, with the right training, right tools, and adapting some extrovert tendencies; those individuals are the highest paid and most successful sales people. That's what sales really is about anyway.

Being YOU

What I do is I empower introverts to step into their power; to use all of who they are in order to be able to really, truly succeed and be a seven figure business owner or professional. They need to have the systems and strategies in place to adapt so they can be more successful.

I tell them first and foremost, don't change who you are.

Learn to use who you are. Don't feed into the BS that you're shy and that you don't have any power and that you don't have anything to add. Being an introvert actually means that you are the one that holds the power and it's time for you to step into your power.

Just as superman has kryptonite, I think that with introverts, the rest of the world, the noise that goes on outside and around all of us is their kryptonite. Knowing that introverts need to schedule time for themselves and to re-charge their battery is the key to embracing their power and living their best life.

Introverts have the natural ability to ask questions, to observe and to do something that often is taken for granted and that is to listen. What we as introverts need to do is leverage who we are.

Speak to Yourself

So I'm going to ask you to do this. Let's do a little role play.

Look at yourself as though you, as a mother, were looking at your child and you saw them standing there staring back. Visualize how you, as a mom, would feel if your child was being seen as shy and not stepping into their power. What would you do or say to help your child be empowered to step into their power? Not to make them be something that they are not, but rather to use the skills that they have to utilize to have the most impact on the world.

Because what we need to understand is that when we as introverts allow ourselves to take a backseat we are actually doing a disservice to the world by not sharing who we are. We are doing them and us a disservice by being something other than who we are or by keeping from the world what we were put on this planet to do. We are keeping from people the words they need to hear by being silent.

And when it comes to accepting the shy label... It's not about being shy. It's about being observant and not needing to be the center of attention. We know as an introvert that we are okay with not needing to have the spotlight. That doesn't mean that we don't need to be seen. Extroverts are going to want to be in the spotlight, whereas an introvert really usually wants to find impactful solutions.

The Right People

So as you build your business, you are going to find as an introvert, that in order to really have the impact that you want, most of the people you are going to surround yourself with are going to be introverts. Now, I don't mean fill your whole business with introverts because that is not going to work. But having a couple of people who you can relate to and who work the same way you do is key. Then, you can sprinkle in a few extroverts for certain things.

You are going to want people who aren't going to suck all the energy out of your room or are constantly needing the spotlight in order to be able to move on. You need to embrace who you are so that you can succeed.

This is going to mean a few things for you. As a business person you are going to spend time with people. As an introvert that means being with people is going to drain your energy. So as a specific on-purpose skill, you need to schedule time for you in your day. Time for meditation or a walk, or other things that you can spend time being alone and re-fueling you. You need to take the time on purpose. Not just accidently get a couple of minutes, but actually schedule in your life time to recharge you. So that you can be as impactful as possible.

A meditation can be a walk. It can be listening to some sort of meditative music. It can be coloring. Having a mandala and spending 15 minutes coloring in an adult coloring book if you will. Because as an introvert, that is where we refuel ourselves. That is where a lot of the creative content comes from. And it's how we don't exhaust or deplete our energy, is by scheduling alone time. It's very easy to run around like a chicken with it's head cut off for 8, 10 or 12 hours a day and not take time for ourselves. But in order to have our most energy and impact as an introvert, we need to initially refuel.

Networking Success

A perfect example managing an introvert's energy goes back to the networking we are talking about. Don't just go to every networking event that there is. You could turn your whole life into a fulltime networking job. DON'T! Instead make a plan. Choose only really good targeted networking events. Pick an event where the people that are going to be there are your ideal clients, partners or businesses. You want to spend your time with the people you want to work with, help, empower and impact. You'll only need a few to be impactful, both in your personal life as well as to your business.

Then when you go to the networking meeting, don't try to meet the whole room. Don't try to have as a goal that if there is 40 or 400 people in the room, that you need to meet all of them. You don't need to get a business card from every single one of them. You need to just set your goal to make sure you meet one or maybe two people and really connecting with them.

Then before you start, before you jump into the room and be an extrovert and try to talk to everybody; take a minute, look around the room, see the room. You may even find that there is another person in the room that is doing just like you are and they are standing back. They may be observing the room or they may be an introvert who hasn't learned yet how to step into their power. It's very likely that this person observing the room is an introvert just like you. They may be exactly the person that you need next in your business and in your life. As you survey the room you will see the people to approach.

This is going to take practice. You are not just going to wake up tomorrow and instantly be good at working in a room full of people. However, as you practice it, you can become comfortable in an group environment because you can put the spotlight on others. You will find that people actually like being around you because you are spotlighting them. You make the person feel important and empowered.

Of course we want to make sure that we are not just spotlighting them. Whether you are in sales, customer service, finance, HR, operations, you've got to master the art of asking questions. You want to learn how to be an excellent communicator so that as you spotlight the person you are talking to in a way that they won't feel like they're in a firing line. But simply that we are interested in them.

Relationships

Here is the truth; introverts have a natural ability to create and maintain long-lasting relationships. It's just really that one little hurdle of meeting people, of being comfortable in a room full of people, that is going to drain your energy. Once you master the skill of being in a room of people you will innately have the ability to really get to know people. Once we do that, we find as introverts that we actually create much deeper bonds with the people we meet.

In the end in business, everything has to do with relationships. Everything that we can do to succeed in our life and in our business is going to come out of the relationships that we have.

By creating kickass relationships, we are creating literally our own tribe. We are creating a group that you can connect with, to help us with things, to help them with things, and to really take our business to the next level.

What's The Cost?

So I'm encouraging you to embrace your introvert nature and step out or step up. If you are in a corporate position, take the opportunity to share your ideas. Often you've been sitting and observing and have ideas. Now is the time to share what you've come up with. If you have a business or if you want to have a business, take the initiative and step out and just do it.

If you don't, what is it going to cost you? What is it going to cost you financially, emotionally, physically, even spiritually for not making the impact that you were put here on the planet to make? What does it cost you when you don't share the things that by listening you have come to realize? You know things. You have answers and solutions. Because you've listened and heard and you know the solution.

If you don't share them, you are literally robbing the company you work for, the business you run, the people that you are in relationships with, of them having a better life. When we don't ask what we need to do to get a promotion. When we don't say, "Hey I want that." How much did that end up costing? What does it cost you financially? What is the emotional impact? What space have you been in? How has emotional stress affected your relationship both personally and professionally? Has your marriage been able to survive? Have you been able to attend your kid's functions? Do you have a good relationship with your children?

When we don't embrace who we are. When we don't take the steps necessary, then these are the things that are going to fall apart. By not sharing we are financially and emotionally stressed. Often our physical health has a tendency to fail. From not eating the right foods, we are either losing or gaining weight. Headaches, backaches, cancers, heart problems, it just goes down the line when we don't step up.

And then there is the spiritual toll. Whether you are religious or not, you have a spirituality about you. So when you are not feeling successful and fulfilled professionally, as well as in life, there is a good chance of not connecting with spirit; which is going to leave a void in your life.

In the end we need to remember that it's never about us. It's about the people that we are here on this planet to impact. We don't want to fall into the trap of being a hider. Squeaking by at work and/or going in the other direction by being an overachiever and killing yourself at work. We simply just want to make an impact. We want to do it so that our business is growing, so that our life is growing and so that we are not holding ourselves back and literally heading towards an implosion in our lives.

If we don't share the things that we've learned, make the impact that we should make, we literally will find everything around us imploding. The thing we need to find is people who can help us evolve and adapt, not into an extrovert but as an introvert. We want people who help us to really, truly embrace who we are.

Making A Difference

Personally, I believe that most people are more afraid of succeeding then failing. They have great ideas. The thing is that they are afraid to voice them because they're afraid that people might actually listen. They are afraid of being seen and then having their nice quiet life interrupted by noise and confusion.

We need as introverts to not hide. We need to not buy into the voice that says:

- Who is going to listen to me?
- How do I articulate it?
- I'm not as outgoing as Johnny, Suzy, Timmy, Sally or Ben.
- Other people seem to have such great ideas and I don't
- Other people have no problems getting what they want
- I'm going to sound stupid.

- I don't have anything of value to offer.
- Who is going to buy what I have to sell or what I have to offer?
- Who is going to take me seriously?

We need to step out and share our ideas, voice them! Give the value that we have. We need to often embrace, especially as an introvert, doing the opposite of what the world is doing. So if the whole world is tweeting or Facebook posting, or running their podcast or any of those things...

There are so many voices out there that my brain hurts. Take for example my iTunes. I subscribe to a person because they've got really good information. Then I find another person with great information. So I load iTunes and I see like 50 updates. 50 things I need to listen to. Then I have to listen or clear them out because they've accumulated. The next day there is 100, and the next day there are 150.

The noise of notifications just keeps building for all of us. There are so many people out there just talking and talking and talking, maybe the most impactful thing we could do is just simply to send one person a handwritten note. When was the last time you got a handwritten note? Imagine how impactful it would be to you for somebody to take the time and sit down and write out a letter to you? Do that for one of your clients and see what kind of impact that makes.

Human Contact

What we need in life is that human contact. And what we as introverts bring back to the world is the ability to connect with other people and create proper communication and contact with people. We have to do it because without us leading the world in listening, communicating and building relationships with people who is going to? It would just be a world full of extroverts out sharing what they have to say. There would be nobody who would ever be emphasizing listening. And nobody would ever get heard.

So think about this again, if somebody sends you a handwritten note, you are going to remember that and you are going to be more inclined to think of that person, whatever their specialty is or whoever they are. They are going to be the first person that comes to your mind in relation to whatever it is they have to offer. Getting on the phone or better yet, if you can sit across the table from them and take the time.

Introverts in business can be so impactful because remember when they connect they connect deeply. They are not just an image on a screen. They are real. When an introvert learns not to hide behind the social media, because it's a cold environment they can form a true and deep connection. So again, what everybody else is doing, you do the complete opposite.

Motivation

Only you can motivate yourself. Only your children can motivate themselves. Only I can motivate myself. I'll give you a prime example and I'll use myself but I'm not the only one that has gone through this. With all the stuff that has happened to me this year, I got depressed. I didn't want to admit it. I didn't want to allow myself to go through the grieving process and I got depressed.

I didn't want to get out of bed in the morning. I would find myself in tears several times throughout the day. I was finding myself not taking action on anything. Not making money. Not cleaning the house. Not doing the laundry. Not doing re-arranging. Not selling things that need to be sold. I was not taking action on anything.

I surrounded myself with some kickass people who are totally, totally awesome and are inspiring, who were doing everything that they could without literally coming to my house and kicking me in the ass. They were doing everything they could to help nudge me along. It didn't work because I was not motivated. I was not motivated to take action. Because in the end only you can motivate you.

With that said, you can find people and things that can

inspire you and go through it with you. If you ae hiding, letting yourself be inspired again is a vital component. It may look like a combination of people. It may look like an accountability partner, somebody else who is in business, or a mentor (and in my professional opinion, mentors are not paid). Mentors are people who help others because they know what it's like to have been in their shoes. There are also some really good people out there that are paid coaches. The coach is someone who is there to listen, support and guide you in the process and make sure you are getting shit done. That is what a coach does. They help you improve your game or business, by two millimeters. Tony Robbins talks about this, but a two millimeter shift in real life or your business can make a significant impact on the amount of money you make, the kind of relationships you have, the outcome of the relationships you have. The happiness in your marriage, your sex life, your kids and your friends and anybody else that is around you.

A Significant Impact

It can be scary for an introvert, I'm not going to lie or sugar-coat it and say that it's going to be unicorns and gumdrops coming out of the sky. It can be scary and it can be nerve-wracking, however if you put the systems in place and you put the strategies in place, if you implement some of the things that I talk about, then what that looks like is more success for your business. You get to spend time taking care of your grandchildren, watching them while you are still young enough to get on the floor and play with them.

If you are in corporate America, success looks like you no longer being passed up for promotions. You will find yourself with opportunities to lead teams and build teams, with opportunities to make a significant impact-- not only from the corporation or company standpoint, but what about the people who are under you. What about being a role model and giving them the support and the guidance that they need, without ruling with an iron fist?

A lot of extroverts (not all), but a lot of extroverts that are in management positions do have more of a tendency to rule with an iron fist and that doesn't work typically as a whole. That does not work in motivating employees and keeping them motivated

If we surround ourselves with people who will inspire us, support us, encourage us, help us, mentor us and yes even sometimes are even coaching us on a specific thing, we can grow. But if we put the systems in place so that we can succeed, we can also not only just succeed ourselves but have all the people around us also be succeeding. We can make an impact in their lives. We can help them really, truly be the best version of themselves.

Because again when people feel heard, they will feel empowered and they will also do better.

A System for Success

We as introverts are great at preparing. So I encourage you to prepare yourself to step out, to be the expert in your field. To use your ability to listen. Listen to your clients. Listen to your employees. Then, you will be able to create a great system for success, success in your business as well as in your life!

Once you have created your plan and done your research, then you can use that information that you've collected to make the impact that you were put here to make. This doesn't mean you stop being you, it just simply means that you take that information and you connect with the people that you can help. An empowered introvert will make self-assured decisions.

In the end it's about having that impact that we were put

here on the world to offer. Empower yourself in the solitude, in the preparation so that you can come out as a winner and you will be a *7-Figure Introvert*. I believe in you. I know you can do it and I appreciate your time reading as I shared. Now, go out and share what you've learned with the world!

Bio Val Neighbors

Val Neighbors is a keynote and breakout speaker working with entrepreneurs to large corporations create a culture of improved sales success, and leadership opportunities.

Val is an introvert by nature who has learned throughout her life how to get comfortable being uncomfortable. It's the readjusting and shifting from introvert to ambivert that has allowed Val to have successful sales careers with companies such as Panasonic and Xerox. She transitioned to the health care industry in the early 2000's creating sales and leadership success for a couple hospice agencies before starting her own company in 2007. Val is part of the 1.8% of women business owners to generate $1 million or more in annual revenue and she accomplished that small feat in just over 24 months.

Val believes everyone breathing is in sales whether they admit to it or not. Val's dynamic personality along with her passion for sales, personal and professional development and strategic planning captivates audiences of all shapes and sizes.

www.ingramcontent.com/pod-product-compliance
Lightning Source LLC
Chambersburg PA
CBHW061445180526
45170CB00004B/1565